THE AI-POWERED PILLOW

Your Solution for Snore-Free Sleep

Matthew H. Larsen

Copyright

About the Author

People in the sleep technology field know Matthew H. Larsen as a genius because he is always coming up with new ideas. He got interested in sleep science because he wanted to find a way to stop snoring, which was making it hard for him to sleep and was also hurting his health in general.

Larsen's academic success was clear from the start, as he graduated from the University of California, Berkeley with a degree in biomedical engineering. He loved combining technology with health remedies. Here, he went into great detail about how sleep works and the subtleties that affect the quality of sleep.

When Larsen joined a new company that was focusing on smart home technology, it was a turning point in his career. The work he did making AI-powered home comfort gadgets showed him that similar technologies could be used to make sleep better. He came up with the idea for the AI-powered pillow that has become associated with his name after this realization.

Larsen is the founder and CEO of RestInnovate, a company whose goal is to improve sleep quality through technology. He bases his methods on solid scientific study, which makes sure that each product not only helps with common sleep problems like snoring but also makes people healthier in general.

Larsen's contribution goes beyond product development. He is a prolific writer and speaker, advocating for greater understanding of sleep health. His articles and talks often focus on the intersection of technology and sleep, stressing the importance of innovative solutions in tackling sleep-related issues.

His successes have not gone unnoticed. Larsen has won numerous awards for his contributions to sleep science and technology. Under his guidance, RestInnovate has been recognized as a pioneering company in the field, setting new standards for what technology can achieve in personal health and well-being.

Matthew H. Larsen's vision for a future where technology seamlessly helps in achieving optimal sleep is more than just a dream. Through his groundbreaking work, he is making it a reality, transforming the way we understand and feel sleep.

Table of content

Introduction

The Dawn of AI in Bedroom Comfort

The introduction of Artificial Intelligence (AI) into the realm of sleep marks a significant leap forward in the pursuit of bedroom comfort and general well-being. AI's entrance into this intimate space of our lives represents more than just a technological improvement; it's a paradigm shift in how we approach rest and rejuvenation.

This revolution started with a simple recognition: sleep, a basic human need, is often disrupted by various factors, many of which have been difficult to address with traditional methods. From snoring to irregular sleep patterns, the difficulties were numerous and complicated. AI, with its ability to learn, adapt, and predict, offered an unprecedented opportunity to tackle these issues in a personalized and efficient way.

The inception of AI in sleep technology took various forms, ranging from smart mattresses and pillows to complex sleep tracking devices. These innovations share a similar goal: to enhance the quality of sleep by understanding the unique needs of each individual. By analyzing sleep patterns, these AI-driven solutions can change the sleeping environment—be it temperature, firmness, or even pillow shape—to ensure optimal rest.

How Technology is Transforming Rest

The transformation of rest through technology is not just about ease; it's about a holistic improvement in health and quality of life. Poor sleep has been linked to a myriad of health problems, from heart disease to cognitive impairment. By improving sleep quality, AI technology is playing a crucial role in preventing these adverse health effects.

One of the most groundbreaking elements of this technological revolution is its ability to provide customized solutions. AI algorithms can learn from a person's sleep habits and make adjustments in real time, giving a level of personalization that was previously unimaginable. This means that the technology can cater to a wide range of sleep-related issues, making it relevant for practically everyone.

Moreover, the integration of AI in sleep technology has opened the door to a deeper knowledge of sleep as a biological process. By collecting and analyzing vast amounts of data, researchers and medical professionals can gain insights into sleep disorders and build more effective treatments.

In sum, the AI revolution in sleep is not just enhancing our nights; it's enriching our days. By ensuring restful sleep, AI is helping us to be more aware, energetic, and mentally sharp. It's an exciting time in the world of sleep science, with AI leading the charge towards a future.

Chapter 1

Unveiling the AI-Powered Pillow

The Genesis of the Snore-Stopping Solution The development of the AI-powered pillow, a groundbreaking innovation in sleep technology, came from a pressing need to address one of the most common sleep disturbances: snoring. Snoring not only affects the quality of sleep for millions of people worldwide but also poses possible health risks and strains personal relationships. The quest to find a non-invasive, effective answer led to the creation of this smart pillow, marking a significant milestone in the journey towards enhancing sleep quality.

This snore-stopping answer was born out of a fusion of advanced sleep science and cutting-edge AI technology. The idea was to create a pillow that could intelligently respond to snoring sounds by changing the sleeper's head position, thus opening airways and alleviating snoring. This idea went through numerous iterations, involving sleep experts, engineers, and AI specialists, who worked to ensure that the pillow not only addressed snoring but also provided optimal comfort and support.

The development method involved rigorous testing and refinement. Prototypes were subjected to various sleep situations to ensure the AI algorithms were precise in detecting and responding to snoring. The team also worked on ensuring the pillow's movements were smooth and subtle, so as not to disturb the sleeper's rest.

Anatomy of a Smart Pillow

At its core, the AI-powered pillow is an epitome of technological complexity wrapped in the simplicity of a pillow. It comprises several key components that work in harmony to provide a smooth sleep experience:

1. **Sensors**:
Embedded within the pillow are smart sensors that monitor sound and movement. These devices are the 'ears' and 'eyes' of the pillow, detecting snoring patterns and the sleeper's position.

2. **AI Processor:**

The heart of the pillow is its AI processor. This miniaturized computer runs algorithms that analyze the data received by the sensors. It's programmed to learn and change to the individual sleeper's habits and needs.

3. **Adjustment Mechanism:**

This is the functional element that gently changes the pillow's shape or position. It's meant to be quiet and smooth, ensuring that the sleeper's rest remains undisturbed even as the pillow works its magic.

4. **Comfort Design:**

Beyond its smart features, the pillow is made for comfort. High-quality materials ensure it is soft yet supportive, ideal for various sleeping positions.

5. Connectivity and Control:

The pillow often features wireless connectivity, allowing for interaction with other smart devices or apps. This allows users to track their sleep patterns, adjust settings, and receive insights into their sleep health.

6. Customizable Settings:

Recognizing that no two sleepers are alike, the pillow is made with customization in mind. Users can change preferences via an app, ensuring the pillow's responses are tailored to their specific needs.

In summary, the AI-powered pillow is more than just a cushion for your head. It's a sophisticated sleep companion that combines the latest in AI technology with the comfort and support of traditional pillows, all while fighting one of the most elusive sleep challenges: snoring. This innovation is not just a testament to human ingenuity but also a beacon of hope for millions wanting a peaceful night's sleep.

Chapter 2

The Science of Sleep and Snoring

Understanding Sleep Patterns

Sleep, a complex and vital process, is more than just a time of rest. It involves various stages, each having a crucial role in our physical and mental well-being. Understanding sleep patterns is key to addressing sleep-related problems like snoring. Typically, sleep is split into two main types: Rapid Eye Movement (REM) and Non-Rapid Eye Movement (NREM). NREM sleep has three stages, each deeper than the last, leading to REM sleep, which is linked with dreaming.

Stage 1 (N1): This is the lightest stage of sleep, where one can be quickly awakened. It acts as a transfer phase from wakefulness to sleep.

Stage 2 (N2): In this stage, the body starts to relax more deeply. It occupies the largest portion of adult sleep and is important for overall rest.

Stage 3 (N3): Often referred to as deep sleep or slow-wave sleep, this stage is important for feeling refreshed. It's during this time that the body repairs and regrows tissues, builds bone and muscle, and strengthens the immune system.

REM Sleep: This stage is marked by rapid eye movement, higher brain activity, and vivid dreams. REM sleep is important for cognitive processes like memory, learning, and Creativity.

Understanding these patterns helps in identifying the stages where snoring commonly occurs, mainly during the deep stages of NREM sleep when the muscles of the throat relax the most.

Decoding the Snore: Causes and Effects

Snoring is the result of the weakening of the throat muscles leading to a partial blockage of the airway. As air passes through the constricted space, it causes the tissues in the throat to vibrate, creating the characteristic snoring sound. The severity and loudness of snoring can vary and are affected by several factors:

1. **Anatomy**:

Individual anatomical differences, such as a narrow throat, enlarged adenoids, or a deviated septum, can add to snoring. These physical traits can cause a narrower air passage, making snoring more likely.

2. **Weight**:

Excess body weight, especially around the neck, can compress and narrow the airways, increasing the chance of snoring.

3. **Age:**

As people age, their throat muscles tend to relax more, which can narrow the passageway and lead to snoring.

4. Lifestyle Factors:

Habits like smoking, alcohol usage, and certain medications can increase muscle relaxation leading to snoring. Furthermore, poor sleep habits and sleep deprivation can also play a part.

5. Sleep Position:

Sleeping on the back can cause the tongue and soft palate to collapse to the back of the mouth, blocking the airway and leading to snoring.

The effects of snoring stretch beyond mere noise disruption. Chronic snoring can lead to fragmented and unrefreshing sleep, adding to daytime fatigue and irritability. It can also be a sign of obstructive sleep apnea (OSA), a more serious disease where the airway repeatedly becomes completely blocked, limiting oxygen flow. OSA is linked with several health risks, including high blood pressure, heart disease, stroke, and diabetes.

Understanding the causes and effects of snoring is important for developing effective interventions. It is here that AI-powered solutions, like the smart pillow, come into play, offering novel approaches to manage and reduce snoring by adapting to individual sleep patterns and behaviors. This not only improves sleep quality but also adds to overall health and well-being.

Chapter 3

How the AI Pillow Works

The Magic Behind AI and Sleep Adjustment The AI Pillow is a marvel of modern technology, blending artificial intelligence with advanced engineering to change sleep. At its core, the pillow uses AI algorithms to process data received from various sensors, adapting in real time to the sleeper's movements, breathing patterns, and snoring sounds.

1. Data Collection: As the user sleeps, embedded devices within the pillow continuously gather data. These include sound sensors to detect snoring, motion sensors to track movements, and pressure sensors to understand sleeping poses.

2. **AI Processing:** The gathered data is fed into the pillow's AI processor. This processor uses machine learning algorithms to study patterns, learning the user's unique sleep behaviors.

3. **Dynamic Adjustment:** Based on the analysis, the pillow starts its adjustment mechanism. If snoring is detected, for instance, the pillow gently shifts the user's head or neck position, allowing better airflow and reducing snoring.

4. **Learning and Adapting:** Over time, the AI system learns from the user's sleep habits, making more accurate and effective

adjustments. It's not just reactive but also predictive, anticipating possible disruptions and mitigating them before they appear.

Sensors and Responses: A Tech Deep Dive Sensors Explained:

1. **Sound Sensors**: Detect the regularity and volume of snoring, differentiating it from other nighttime sounds.

2. **Motion Sensors**: Monitor movements such as tossing and turning, aligning the pillow properly for optimal comfort.

3. **Pressure Sensors**: Map the pressure spread of the head and neck, ensuring proper alignment.

4. **Automatic Re-positioning**: The pillow can gently reposition itself to maintain the most effective angle for airway openness and comfort.

5. **Firmness Adjustment**: Certain models can change their firmness, becoming softer or firmer as needed to provide the best support.

The AI pillow can integrate with other smart devices or apps, providing feedback on sleep quality and offering suggestions for improvement.

Privacy and Security: Considering the personal nature of the data gathered, these pillows are designed with robust security measures to protect user privacy.

Chapter 4

Benefits Beyond Snore Prevention

Enhancing Sleep Quality

The AI-powered pillow, while mainly designed to address snoring, offers a range of benefits that significantly enhance overall sleep quality. These benefits stem from the pillow's ability to provide personalized warmth and support, adapting to the individual's sleeping habits and physical needs.

1. Improved Sleep Architecture:

By reducing snoring and adjusting to optimal positions, the pillow helps keep a stable sleep routine. This means fewer awakenings and disruptions, allowing for more regular cycles of REM and deep NREM sleep, which are crucial for restorative rest.

2. Optimal Neck and Spine Alignment:

The pillow's adjustable features ensure that the neck and spine are properly aligned. This reduces the risk of developing neck pain and headaches, common issues linked with poor sleeping posture.

3. Enhanced Comfort:

The AI pillow's ability to change its firmness and shape based on the sleeper's movements and preferred sleeping position adds to a more comfortable and satisfying sleep experience.

4. Better Sleep Environment:

Some AI pillows are equipped with features like temperature control, which can further enhance sleep quality by keeping a comfortable sleeping environment throughout the night.

Health and Wellness Advantages

The advantages of the AI-powered pillow stretch into broader aspects of health and wellness. Good quality sleep is foundational to overall health, and by enhancing sleep quality, the pillow indirectly adds to various health benefits.

1. **Mental Health Benefits:**

Improved sleep quality can lead to better mood regulation, reduced stress, and a lower chance of depression and anxiety. Adequate rest is important for cognitive processes like memory, concentration, and decision-making.

2. **Physical Health Benefits:**

Consistently good sleep helps regulate body weight, strengthens the immune system, and reduces the chance of chronic diseases such as heart disease, diabetes, and hypertension.

3. **Increased Daytime Energy and Productivity:**

Better sleep leads to increased awareness and energy levels during the day. This can result in higher productivity, better success at work or school, and an overall more active lifestyle.

4. Long-Term Health Effects:

Over time, the cumulative effect of improved sleep can be important. It can play a part in longevity, quality of life, and the prevention of age-related diseases.

In conclusion, the AI-powered pillow is not just a tool for snoring prevention; it is a comprehensive sleep aid that offers a multitude of benefits for both sleep quality and general health and wellness. Its innovative design and technology mark a major step forward in the quest for better sleep and, by extension, a healthier life.

Chapter 5

User Experiences and Success Stories

Real-Life Transformations

The AI-powered pillow has been a game-changer in the lives of many users, bringing about real-life changes that go beyond mere snoring solutions. These stories often highlight the profound effect that improved sleep quality can have on various aspects of life.

From Restless Nights to Refreshed Mornings:

Many users claim a drastic change in their sleep patterns. Previously plagued by restless nights due to snoring and discomfort, they now enjoy uninterrupted sleep and wake up feeling refreshed and energetic.

Enhanced Relationship Dynamics:

For couples, the reduction of snoring has had a significant positive effect on their relationships. Partners who had to sleep separately due to loud snoring have reunited, leading to better intimacy and emotional bonds.

Boost in Daytime Productivity:

With better sleep quality, users often report a noticeable increase in their daytime energy and concentration levels. This has led to improved productivity at work and a more active lifestyle.

Health Improvements:

Individuals with chronic health problems linked to poor sleep have seen notable improvements. Reduction in sleep disturbances has led to better management of conditions like hypertension and diabetes, and general enhancements in physical and mental well-being.

Testimonials: Before and After

Testimonials from users often paint a vivid picture of the before-and-after situations, showcasing the transformative power of the AI-powered pillow.

1. John, a Long-time Snorer: "Before using the AI pillow, my snoring was so bad that it kept my wife awake at night. We tried

everything, but nothing worked. Since I started using this pillow, my snoring has greatly reduced. My wife and I are sleeping in the same room again, and we both wake up feeling well-rested."

2. Emma, Struggling with Neck Pain: "I used to wake up with neck pain almost every morning. I thought it was just something I had to live with. But after moving to this smart pillow, which adjusts to support my neck, the pain is gone. I'm sleeping better and no longer dread going to bed."

3. Alex, a Shift Worker: "Working odd hours meant my sleep was all over the place. The AI pillow's ability to adapt to my erratic sleep routine has been a lifesaver. I'm falling

asleep faster and getting more quality sleep, which is amazing."

4. Sara, a Health Enthusiast: "As someone who is very health-conscious, I'm amazed at the change good sleep has made. My energy levels are higher, I'm more focused during workouts, and my general mood has improved. This pillow hasn't just changed how I sleep; it's changed how I live."

These stories and testimonials underscore the profound effect that the AI-powered pillow has had on its users. By addressing a common yet often ignored problem like snoring and sleep discomfort, this innovation has greatly improved the state of life for many individuals.

Chapter 6

Comparative Analysis with Traditional Pillows

What Sets the AI Pillow Apart?

The AI-powered pillow represents a significant advancement over traditional pillows, mainly due to its integration of technology for personalized sleep enhancement. Here are key features that set it apart:

1. Adaptive Support:

Unlike traditional pillows, which have a set shape and firmness, AI pillows can adapt in real-time to the user's sleeping position, movements, and even breathing patterns. This provides optimal alignment and comfort throughout the night.

2. Snoring Mitigation:

The most distinguishing feature of the AI pillow is its ability to recognise and respond to snoring. By subtly adjusting the user's head position, it helps keep an open airway, something traditional pillows can't do.

3. Sleep Data Analysis:

AI pillows often come with sensors that collect data on sleep quality, including length, disturbances, and patterns. This information can be used to further adjust the sleeping experience.

4. Smart Home Integration:

Many AI pillows offer connectivity with other smart devices, allowing for a more integrated sleep experience. For example, they can work in tandem with smart thermostats to control bedroom temperature for optimal sleep conditions.

5. Durability and Maintenance:
While traditional pillows require regular replacement, AI pillows are built with durability in mind. They also often feature materials that are easy to clean and keep

The Old vs. The New: A Comprehensive Look

Traditional Pillows:

1. Comfort: Based on material (feather, foam, etc.), but does not adapt to changes in sleep position.

2. Health Benefits: Limited to giving basic neck support, with no capabilities to address specific health issues like snoring.

3. Maintenance: Requires regular repair; material quality degrades over time.

4. Technology: No technological integration; simply a physical support item.

5. Cost: Generally cheaper with a wide range of options offered.

AI Pillows

1. Comfort: Dynamically adapts to provide personalized support, improving comfort throughout the night.

2. Health Benefits: Actively works to reduce snoring and can possibly improve overall sleep quality, having indirect health benefits.

3. Maintenance: Built for durability with advanced materials; often easy to clean and keep.

4. Technology: Embedded with sensors and AI algorithms for sleep tracking and automatic adjustments.

5. Cost: More expensive due to the addition of advanced technology.

In conclusion, while traditional pillows provide basic comfort, AI pillows offer a complete solution that not only improves sleep quality but also adds to better health and well-being. They represent a leap forward in sleep technology, aligning with the needs of a modern, health-conscious society.

Chapter 7

Maintenance, Care, and Durability

Keeping Your Smart Pillow in Top Shape
The AI-powered pillow, with its advanced technology and materials, needs specific care to ensure its longevity and performance. Proper upkeep is key to keeping it in top shape.

Cleaning and Hygiene:

Most AI pillows come with a replaceable and washable cover, making it easy to keep clean. It's important to follow the manufacturer's instructions regarding washing and drying to avoid damage to the materials and embedded sensors.

Battery and Power Management:

If the pillow includes electronic components or sensors that require charging, it's essential to follow a regular charging routine to keep battery health. Avoid overcharging and fully draining the battery to extend its life.

Firmware Updates:

Like any smart gadget, the AI pillow may receive firmware updates to improve functionality or fix bugs. Keeping the pillow updated ensures you benefit from the latest features and changes.

Storage:

When not in use, store the pillow in a cool, dry place away from direct sunlight to avoid damage to its electronic components and fabric.

Handling and Use:

While made for durability, it's important to handle the pillow with care. Avoid excessive force or bending of the pillow, especially in areas where sensors or electronic components are housed.

Longevity and Reliability Assessments

1. Material Quality:

AI pillows are usually made with high-quality materials designed to withstand regular use while retaining their shape and functionality. This includes durable outer fabrics and interior components that are resistant to wear and tear.

2. **Electronic Component Durability:**

The electronic and AI components are tested for durability under different conditions. However, like any electronic device, they may finally need replacement or repair.

3. **Warranty and Support:**

Most makers offer a warranty for the AI pillow, covering defects in materials and workmanship. It's important to understand the guarantee terms and what is covered. Additionally, customer help can provide guidance on care and troubleshooting.

4. **Long-Term Performance:**

Over time, the performance of the AI features, like any technology, may lessen. Regular updates and good maintenance practices can help in preserving its functioning.

5. User Feedback and Reviews:

Regularly checking user feedback and reviews can provide insights into common problems or maintenance tips, helping to extend the pillow's life.

In summary, the AI-powered pillow, with its blend of technology and comfort, demands a slightly different approach to maintenance than standard pillows. Proper care and regular updates are crucial to ensure its longevity and reliability, allowing users to enjoy the benefits of better sleep quality for years to come.

Chapter 8

Future of Sleep Technology

What's Next in AI-Powered Bedding?

The horizon of AI-powered bedding is expanding quickly, promising innovative developments that aim to revolutionize the way we sleep. Here are some of the expected advancements:

1.   Holistic   Sleep   Environment Management:

Future AI bedding could extend its powers to manage the entire sleep environment, including lighting, temperature, and sound. Imagine a bed that adjusts its firmness based on your sleep stage or a room that changes its environmental settings for optimal sleep conditions.

2. Advanced Biometric Monitoring:

Beyond basic sleep tracking, future AI bedding may add more advanced biometric sensors to monitor vital signs like heart rate, blood oxygen levels, and even stress markers. This could be particularly helpful for monitoring and managing health conditions.

3. Personalized Sleep Coaching:

With the influx of data from advanced monitoring, AI can grow into a personal sleep coach. By analyzing sleep patterns over time, it could provide tailored tips on lifestyle changes, sleep habits, and even diet guidance to improve sleep quality.

4. **Integration with Health Platforms**:

As health and wellness become more connected, AI-powered bedding could easily integrate with other health platforms and devices, sharing data to provide a complete view of an individual's health.

5. **Responsive Sleep Aids:**

Future bedding could include responsive elements like automatically adjusting pillows or mattresses that change their structure to relieve pressure points, align the spine properly, or even gently wake you up at the optimal time in your sleep cycle.

Emerging Trends and Future Predictions

Sustainable and Eco-friendly Materials: With growing environmental concerns, the future of sleep technology is likely to see a shift towards sustainable and biodegradable materials, reducing the ecological impact of bedding products.

Machine Learning and AI Advances: As machine learning algorithms become more complex, the precision and effectiveness of AI in sleep technology will continue to improve, offering more nuanced and effective sleep solutions.

Wearable combination: The combination of AI bedding with wearable technology, such as smartwatches and fitness trackers, could provide a more holistic approach to sleep management.

Smart Fabrics: The development of smart fabrics with embedded sensors could lead to bedding that can not only track sleep but also provide therapeutic benefits such as muscle relaxation or heat treatment.

Virtual Reality (VR) and Augmented Reality (AR) Applications: VR and AR could be used in tandem with sleep technology for relaxation and stress reduction, offering immersive experiences that promote faster and deeper sleep.

In summary, the future of sleep technology, especially in the realm of AI-powered bedding, is set to not only improve the quality of sleep but also integrate it more closely with overall health and wellness. These advancements are expected to change sleep from a passive state to an actively managed and vital component of our daily health regimen.

Conclusion

A Recap of the AI Pillow's Impact

The journey of the AI-powered pillow, from its conceptualization to its broad adoption, marks a significant milestone in the quest for restful sleep. This innovative tool has revolutionized the way we view and interact with our sleeping environments. By integrating cutting-edge AI technology with the traditional idea of a pillow, it has addressed one of the most common and frustrating sleep disturbances: snoring.

The AI pillow's ability to adapt to individual sleeping habits, adjust head positioning to open up airways, and provide personalized comfort has transformed the sleep experience for many. Its effect goes beyond just mitigating snoring; it enhances overall sleep quality, aligns the spine correctly, and contributes to better physical and mental health.

Final Thoughts on the Snore-Free Revolution

The snore-free revolution brought about by the AI pillow is just the beginning of a bigger movement towards smarter, health-focused sleep solutions. As we continue to accept technology in our daily lives, the integration of AI into our sleep routines is a natural progression. This innovation is a testament to the potential of technology to improve not just the quality of our sleep but also our general well-being.

Looking forward, the opportunities in sleep technology are boundless. With ongoing advancements in AI and machine learning, the future offers more personalized, effective, and holistic approaches to sleep management. The potential benefits of these developments are enormous, ranging from enhanced personal health and wellness to broader implications for public health and productivity.

In conclusion, the AI-powered pillow represents more than just a technology breakthrough; it symbolizes a shift in our approach to sleep — from passive to proactive, from one-size-fits-all to highly personalized. As we continue to explore and innovate in this field, we move closer to a future where restful, rejuvenating sleep is

available to all, paving the way for healthier,
happier lives.